FULL SPEED AHEAD!

HOW FAST THINGS GO

BY CRUSCHIFORM

ABRAMS BOOKS FOR YOUNG READERS, NEW YORK

0.3 KM/H
0.2 MPH

1 Sea horse 2 Galápagos tortoise

1

2

1 Hedgehog 2 Millipede

1

2

1 *Tegenaria* spider 2 Excavator 3 A person walking

1 The caravel *Santa Maria* 2 Roller skates 3 Carp
4 Basilisk lizard 5 Elephant 6 Stagecoach

20 KM/H
12 MPH

1 Skydiver 2 Camel 3 Hornet
4 Bicycle 5 Viking longship

35 KM/H
22 MPH

1 Alligator
2 USS *Nautilus* nuclear submarine

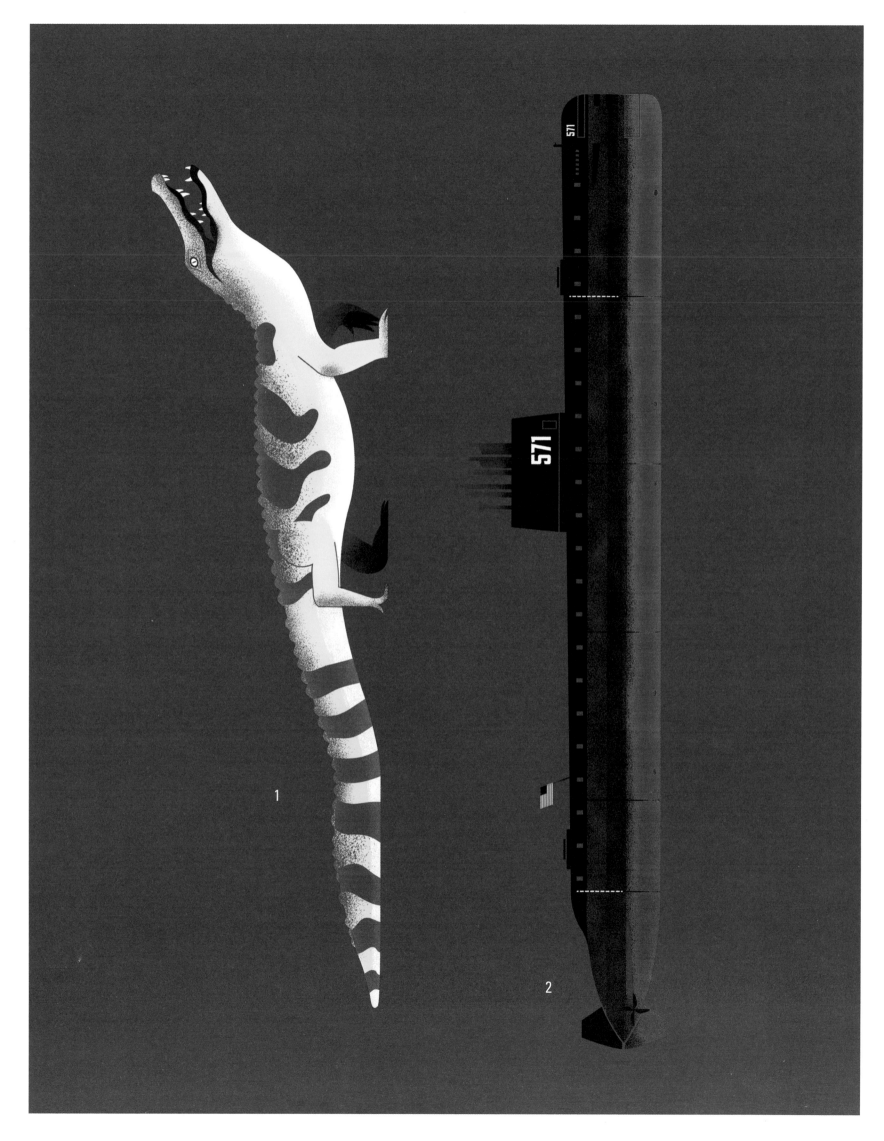

1 The ocean liner *Normandie* 2 Blue whale 3 The ocean liner *Queen Mary II*
4 Cargo ship 5 Motor scooter 6 Montgolfier hot-air balloon 7 Mouflon

1 NORMANDIE

3 QUEEN MARY 2

4 P&O NEDLLOYD INC.

70 KM/H
43 MPH

1 Hare 2 Sessa C68 yacht 3 Greyhound
4 Leclerc tank 5 Racehorse 6 The *Orient-Express* steam train

1 Zodiac inflatable boat 2 Sphinx moth 3 Pheasant

90 KM/H
56 MPH

1 Springbok antelope 2 Dragonfly 3 Sailboard
4 Mako shark 5 Fire truck

110 KM/H
68 MPH

1 Cheetah 2 The electric car *Jamais-Contente* 3 Dauphine car
4 Farman MF 11BIS biplane 5 Indo-Pacific sailfish

1 The zeppelin *Hindenburg* 2 Motorcycle

1 Swift 2 Hughes MD 500 helicopter

1 Caudron Simoun touring plane 2 Downhill skier 3 Tennis ball

350 KM/H
217 MPH

1 High-speed train 2 Peregrine falcon 3 Frigate bird 4 Formula 1 racecar

Tornado

1 *The Blue Flame* rocket car 2 Passenger jet
3 *Thrust SSC* turbojet car

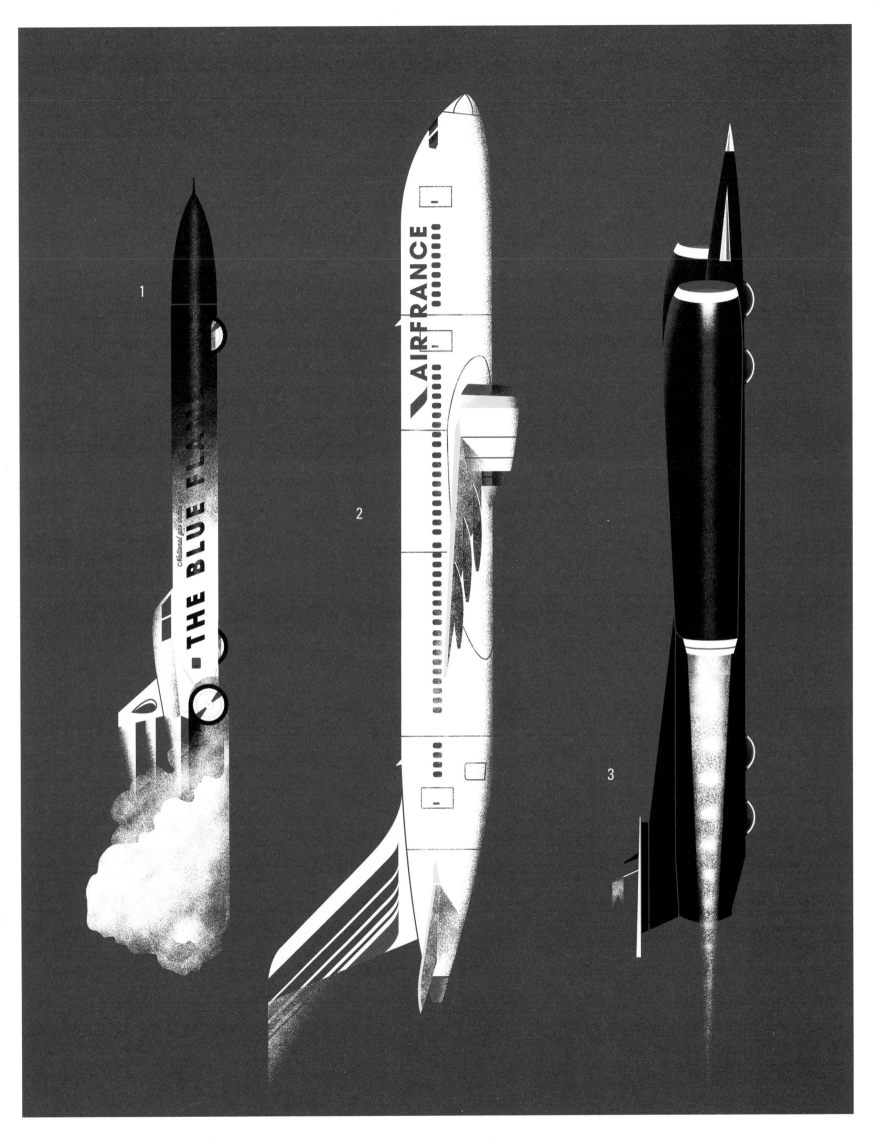

1 Bullet 2 The Earth's rotation

Blackbird spy plane

40,000 KM/H

25,000 MPH

Apollo 11 spacecraft

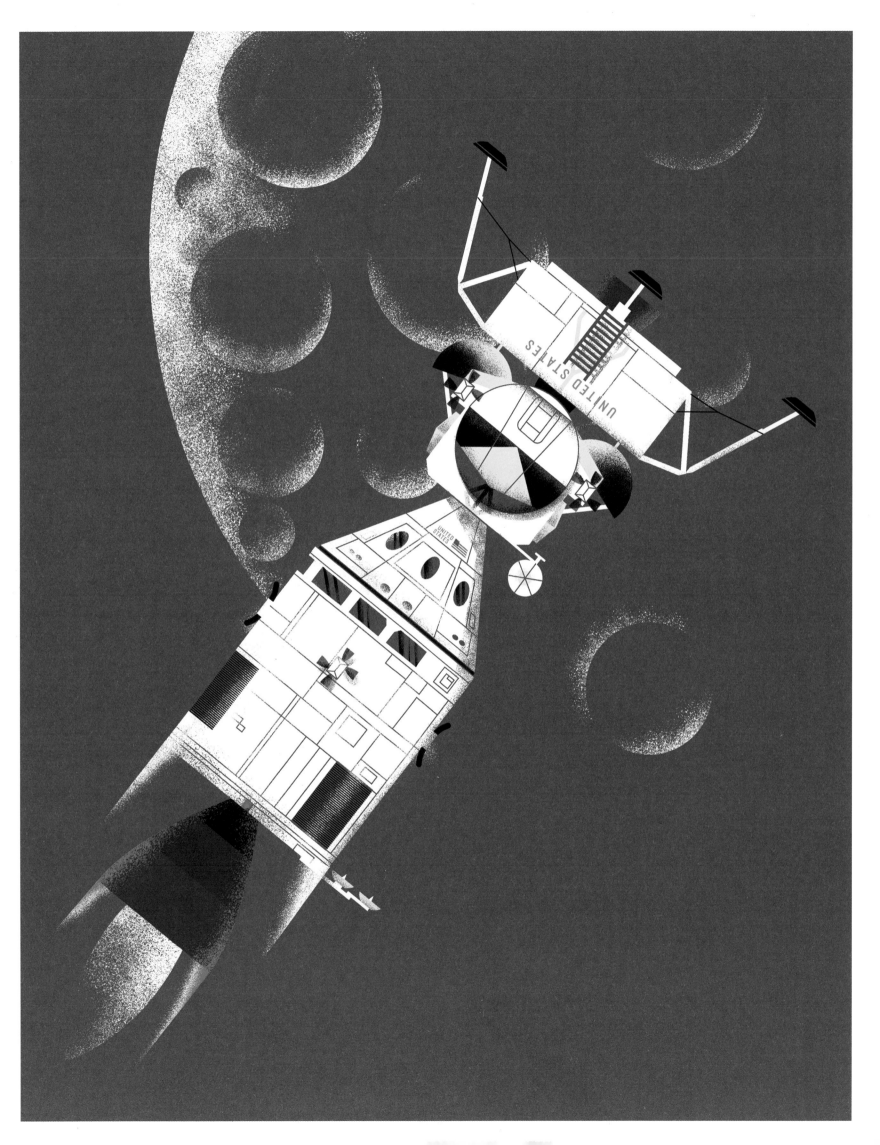

Shooting star

GLOSSARY

What is speed?
It's the relationship between distance and time.

In the sixteenth century, when Matteo Ricci—an Italian Jesuit missionary who was the first European to settle in Beijing, China—wrote to his family back home, it took nine years for his letters to reach them. Now when we send a written message from Beijing to Italy, it arrives in less than a minute. The distance is still the same, but the time it takes the news to travel is shorter.

In the twenty-first century, the speed with which you can get from New York City to Washington, D.C., depends on whether you drive a car, ride on a train, or fly in a plane. Washington is still the same distance from New York, but the duration of the trip changes, based on the speed of your chosen method of transport.

SEA HORSE

The sea horse is an unusual little fish. At most 6 inches (16 cm) long, it resembles a knight from a chess set. It waits in ambush to catch its prey—tiny little animals called zooplankton. The sea horse has a maximum speed of 980 feet per hour (300 meters per hour).

GALÁPAGOS TORTOISE

The Galápagos tortoise is an impressive reptile. A true giant tortoise, it can weigh up to 880 pounds (400 kg), measure nearly 7 feet (2 m) long, and live nearly 200 years. For two hours every day, it warms itself in the sun, so its shell can absorb the energy. The Galápagos tortoise moves very slowly, rarely going above 1,200 feet per hour (370 meters per hour).

HEDGEHOG

The hedgehog is a small mammal found in Europe, Asia, and Africa. It is equally at home in deserts, farmland, and tropical forests. A nocturnal animal, it sets out at dusk to hunt, burrow, and climb in search of food. It can move at a speed of 1.1 mph (1.8 km/h), and if it is frightened by a predator, it rolls itself up in a ball and sticks out its spines.

MILLIPEDE

The millipede possesses an impressive number of feet. Certain species have as many as 750 feet and measure more than 15 inches (38 cm) in length. Millipedes are found mostly in humid places, under rocks, in the soil, and in dead wood. When they feel threatened, they roll themselves up into a spiral for protection. They can also run away—but not faster than 1.1 mph (1.8 km/h).

TEGENARIA SPIDER

Spiders of the genus *Tegenaria* are some of the most common house spiders. Some are among the largest spiders in Europe, at up to 5 inches (13 cm). That's nothing compared with the South American Goliath spider, which measures nearly 1 foot (30 cm)! They are also among the fastest, recorded at 2.2 mph (3.5 km/h). Nevertheless, they're harmless to humans.

EXCAVATOR

A smaller version of a steam shovel, an excavator is a construction machine used primarily in demolition and in the extraction of materials, thanks to its articulated arm and its bucket. Equipped with tracks, the excavator moves at 2.5 mph (4 km/h), and when outfitted with tires, it can get up to 25 mph (40 km/h), or the speed of a wild rabbit.

A PERSON WALKING

One of the physical characteristics of *Homo sapiens* (that is, us) is that we are bipedal—"two-footed." People have walked upright for about 1.5 million years. Following a study on human movement, a "normal" walking pace was determined to be around 2 mph (3 km/h). A deliberate walking pace is around 2.5 mph (4 km/h), and a fast pace is around 3 mph (5 km/h).

THE CARAVEL *SANTA MARIA*

A caravel is a sailing ship with tall sides that was invented by the Portuguese at the beginning of the fifteenth century, primarily for transporting merchandise. The design was quickly adopted in most Mediterranean countries, thanks to its lightness and its speed of 4.5 knots, or 5.2 mph (8.3 km/h)—which was fast for the time! In 1492, the famous navigator Christopher Columbus set sail aboard a caravel, the *Santa Maria*, to discover the Americas.

ROLLER SKATES

The invention of roller skates dates to the eighteenth century. At the time, they were made of wood and were attached to shoes. Over the centuries they've evolved from four wheels on two axles (the quad) to three, four, or five wheels in a line. Roller skates allow a person to go 7 mph (12 km/h) on flat ground. They're used in different sports, such as hockey and roller derby.

CARP

The carp is a freshwater fish native to Europe and Asia. Renowned for its longevity, it can live up to thirty years. Sure, it doesn't swim very fast (7 mph [12 km/h]), but it's aggressive and robust, which enables it to swim upstream through rivers and waterfalls to reproduce. It is a symbol of perseverance in Chinese culture.

BASILISK LIZARD

Measuring between 23 and 30 inches (60 and 75 cm), the basilisk is a large but very agile and light lizard found in the tropical forests of the Americas. A solitary creature, it lives near running water, eating small animals and insects. When the basilisk needs to make a quick getaway, it stands on its hind legs and runs in long strides on water, at a speed of 7 mph (12 km/h), which is how it gets its nickname: the Jesus Christ lizard.

ELEPHANT

Weighing more than 6 tons (5,400 kg), the elephant is the largest land mammal in the world. Found in areas of Africa and Asia, elephants are social animals that live in communities. As part of a herd, an elephant walks at nearly 6 mph (10 km/h) and can cover nearly 50 miles (80 km) a day in the search for new pastures. But the moment it feels threatened, it can charge its predator at a top speed of 25 mph (40 km/h).

STAGECOACH

At the beginning of the nineteenth century, vehicles pulled by animals were the principal mode of long-distance travel. While cattle were used to work the fields, horses pulled stagecoaches. Generally equipped with two to four horses, these carriages could transport up to fifteen passengers. Long and tiring trips (at an average speed of 6 mph [10 km/h]) necessitated a stop about every 12 miles (20 km) to change teams of horses. At the time, it took two days to get from New York to Philadelphia.

SKYDIVER

When skydivers jump out of a plane that's flying at an altitude of more than 3,300 feet (1,000 m), they fall at a rate of nearly 125 mph (200 km/h). When they open their parachutes, they slow immediately, traveling at a rate of 12 mph (20 km/h). They can then take the time to contemplate the landscape below them before touching down.

CAMEL

Native to central Asia, the Bactrian camel is a surprising mammal. With its two humps, which serve as energy stores, it can go for long periods of time without food in the extreme climate of the desert, and it can reach a top speed of 16 mph (25 km/h). Its larger, more muscular cousin the dromedary camel, which has only one hump, can reach a speed of 56 mph (90 km/h)!

HORNET

The hornet is an insect found all over the world. It is a fearsome predator of wasps, bees, and flies, thanks to its large size (1.7 inches [4.4 cm]), its powerful venom, and also its flight speed—the maximum recorded by scientists is 13.2 mph (21.2 km/h).

BICYCLE

It was in the 1860s that the first pedal velocipede (an early kind of bicycle) saw the light of day in France. It was immediately immensely popular. By 1890, the bicycle had become very much like the ones we ride today. And it became, in the space of a century, the most popular method of transportation in the world, allowing riders to get around at an average speed of 12 mph (20 km/h). On a racing bike, a cyclist can go as fast as 43 mph (70 km/h), or the speed of a racehorse.

VIKING LONGSHIP

The longship was the preeminent ship of conquest for the Vikings, a great warlike and seafaring people of Scandinavia from the eighth century to the thirteenth century. This ship, with its large sail and its team of oarsmen, was both light and sturdy. It could achieve an average speed of 13 knots, or 15 mph (24 km/h), and cover more than 90 miles (150 km) a day on long expeditions.

ALLIGATOR

The alligator is a cold-blooded amphibian reptile. A solitary creature that doesn't move around much, it lives in swamps and on lakeshores in the south-eastern United States. It can measure up to 16 feet (5 m) long and can weigh more than 800 pounds (360 kg). Despite its bulk and its slow metabolism, an alligator can attack prey at 24 mph (38 km/h) over short distances, which makes it a fearsome predator.

USS *NAUTILUS* NUCLEAR SUBMARINE

Taking its name from Jules Verne's famous novel *20,000 Leagues Under the Sea*, the USS *Nautilus*, a U.S. Navy attack sub built in the 1950s, was the world's first nuclear-powered vessel. It was equipped with six torpedo tubes, and it measured 344 feet (105 m) long and only 28 feet (8.5 m) wide. It could accommodate a crew of ninety-six and stay submerged for weeks at a time, traveling at an average speed of 20 knots, or 23 mph (37 km/h).

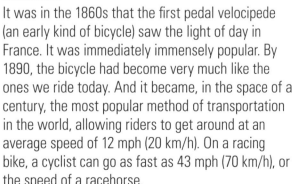

THE OCEAN LINER *NORMANDIE*

The *Normandie* was a French transatlantic ocean liner in service from 1935 to 1942. It made the crossing from Le Havre, France, to New York City in six days. The largest and most beautiful liner of its time, it was a symbol of French luxury and refinement in the 1930s. Measuring 1,029 feet (313 m) long, it could carry two thousand passengers and reach a speed of 30 knots, or 35 mph (56 km/h), thanks to its four turboelectric motors.

BLUE WHALE

The blue whale is the largest marine mammal in the world. It can weigh up to 165 tons (150,000 kg) and measure up to 115 feet (35 m) in length, or taller than a ten-story building. While its cruising speed is only about 12 mph (20 km/h)—which is to say, no faster than a person on a bicycle—it can reach up to 30 mph (50 km/h) in short bursts.

THE OCEAN LINER *QUEEN MARY II*

A British transatlantic ocean liner launched in 2004 and still in service, the *Queen Mary II* measures 1,131 feet (345 m) long and 236 feet (72 m) tall. It is equipped with five swimming pools, eight Jacuzzis, twenty restaurants, a theater, a casino, and a nightclub. It can carry three thousand passengers at a cruising speed of 28.5 knots, or 33 mph (52 km/h), thanks to its gas turbines and its powerful diesel motors.

MOUFLON

The mouflon, a wild mountain sheep, is found at high altitudes on mountainsides in Europe, western Asia, and Africa. Capable of moving with agility on steep, rocky slopes, it can reach speeds in excess of 37 mph (60 km/h).

CARGO SHIP

From ancient times until the mid-nineteenth century, ships essentially moved under the power of the wind, harnessed by sails. But the invention of steam-powered propellers during the Industrial Revolution turned naval construction on its head. The cargo ship, first introduced in the 1970s, is a vessel specifically designed to transport merchandise. Today it is the principal maritime freight transport. Equipped with diesel motors, the container ship moves at an average speed of 24 knots, or 28 mph (45 km/h).

MOTOR SCOOTER

A motor scooter is a kind of motorcycle with small wheels and a seat that allows one to sit atop it rather than astride it. The Vespa—the most recognizable scooter—started production in 1946 and was a major fad in the 1950s. Still very popular today, particularly in Europe and in certain Asian countries, the Vespa is a symbol of freedom and independence, and can exceed a speed of 62 mph (100 km/h), though in cities the speed limit is closer to 30 mph (50 km/h).

MONTGOLFIER HOT-AIR BALLOON

The Montgolfier was a hot-air balloon named for the brothers who invented it in 1782. Its first flight with "passengers" (a sheep, a rooster, and a duck) was made in front of the court of King Louis XVI of France. The Montgolfier ascended into the sky by sending hot air up into the balloon, which made it lighter than air. While its cruising speed varied depending on wind currents, the Montgolfier could reach a speed of up to 30 mph (50 km/h).

HARE

The hare is a wild rabbit found throughout most continents, on cultivated plains, deserts, scrubland, tundra, and moors. Slender and light, the hare is characterized by long, muscular hind legs that allow it to move in great bounds when chased by a predator. In such circumstances, it can move at 43 mph (70 km/h) and jump more than 6 feet (2 m) in the air.

SESSA C68 YACHT

A yacht is a pleasure craft about 65 feet (20 m) long that is used primarily for leisure cruises and is powered by propellers. The Sessa C68 is a luxury yacht outfitted for maximum comfort. Particularly powerful, it can get up to a speed of 38 knots, or 44 mph (72 km/h).

GREYHOUND

The greyhound is a powerful and very fast racing dog originally from Great Britain. Since 1750, the British aristocracy has raised greyhounds, not just for hunting but also for races in which a hare or a pheasant is chased by the dogs. Today, betting on dog races is popular in Britain and elsewhere, though the rabbits and pheasants have been replaced by artificial lures. At the dog track, one can see dogs running at nearly 43 mph (70 km/h).

LECLERC TANK

The Leclerc tank, which takes its name from a famous general, is a French battle tank in current use. The first armored all-terrain vehicles, which saw combat during World War I, were powered by gas motors. Over time, these motors were replaced by gas turbines that were more powerful and posed less of a risk of fire. Outfitted with tracks, the Leclerc can operate on all types of terrain and can reach a speed of 45 mph (72 km/h) on roads.

RACEHORSE

Called "the most noble of man's conquests," the horse has long been used for transportation, labor, and warfare . . . and also entertainment. Since ancient times, equestrian sports have been a popular pastime. After World War II, the selective breeding of pure-blood racehorses saw a boost in popularity in the United States. Known for their speed and agility, racehorses can reach speeds approaching 43 mph (70 km/h) over short distances.

THE *ORIENT-EXPRESS* STEAM TRAIN

Around 1830, the discovery of steam propulsion ushered in great progress in the realm of transportation. Little by little, the steam locomotive replaced animal power, and numerous railroads were built across Europe. The luxury train the *Orient Express*, which began service in 1883, connected Paris, France, with Istanbul (which was called Constantinople at the time), in Turkey, in fewer than five days, making it the fastest train at the time. Over the years, the *Orient Express* came to settle on an average speed of 43 mph (70 km/h).

80 KM/H
50 MPH

ZODIAC INFLATABLE BOAT

The Zodiac is a very light boat made of rubber and powered by an outboard motor. Able to hold between two and ten people, it is primarily used by the navy and the marines as a rescue vehicle and landing craft. Thanks to its structure, it can weather rough seas and can reach a top speed of 45 knots, or 52 mph (83 km/h).

SPHINX MOTH

The sphinx is a large moth with a tapered body and long wings with a span of 1.4 to 6 inches (3.5 to 15 cm). Certain species of sphinx moths can fly at more than 30 mph (50 km/h) and can cover great distances over the course of their lives (which last from 10 to 25 days). Scientists clocked the sphinx moth's speed record at more than 49.8 mph (80.2 km/h).

PHEASANT

The pheasant is a bird that lives in groves and on the outskirts of forests in low-lying areas. In the seventeenth century, pheasant hunting was a popular sport among the European aristocracy, who often used hounds to chase the birds. The wild pheasant can flee its predators at a high speed in excess of 50 mph (80 km/h).

90 KM/H
56 MPH

SPRINGBOK ANTELOPE

The springbok is a small antelope that lives in the steppes and the rocky deserts of southern Africa. Very fast and agile, it can sprint at 60 mph (95 km/h), in bounds of up to 10 feet (3 m) high and 50 feet (15 m) long, which allows it to escape its predators, which include lions and leopards. However, it can only cover about half a mile (800 m) at such a speed.

DRAGONFLY

The dragonfly is an insect that lives on the banks of bodies of stagnant freshwater. Its characteristic wings, which move independently of one another, allow it to do things other insects can't: hover, fly backward, and take off vertically. While a hornet can't go faster than 14 mph (22 km/h), dragonflies have been clocked at 60.4 mph (97.2 km/h)!

SAILBOARD

Halfway between sailing and surfing, windsurfing is a sport that can be practiced in calm or vigorous water. The speed you can get up to on a sailboard depends quite a lot on weather conditions and on the wind. A speed record was clocked at nearly 49 knots, or 56 mph (90 km/h), nearly twice as fast as an ocean liner.

MAKO SHARK

The mako shark is found in shallow, temperate waters in most of the world's oceans. Its particularly hydrodynamic movement and its large size (13 feet [4 m]) make the mako a very fast swimmer whose speed is around 47 mph (75 km/h). It is also capable of launching itself like a torpedo at its prey—at nearly 56 mph (90 km/h)—and can even jump out of the water at it, to a height of 20 feet (6 m)!

FIRE TRUCK

Firefighters put out fires and administer emergency medical care. They use a variety of specialized vehicles for different situations: the fire engine, the ambulance, the hook and ladder. While the speed limit in cities is much lower than 56 mph (90 km/h), fire trucks are authorized to move as quickly as necessary in order to arrive on the scene faster. .

110 KM/H
68 MPH

CHEETAH

A solitary predator on the steppes and savannas of Africa, the cheetah is an excellent hunter. It is capable of reaching a top speed of 68 mph (110 km/h), though only over short distances (660 feet [200 m]), because the exertion tires it out. It is nevertheless the fastest land animal in the world!

THE ELECTRIC CAR *JAMAIS-CONTENTE*

The *Jamais-Contente* (French for "Never Satisfied") was the first automobile to break the 100 km/h (62 mph) barrier. This electric car, shaped like an artillery shell, was built in 1899 with materials that were very innovative for the time: aluminum alloy for the body and rubber for the tires. Driven by its inventor, Camille Jenatzy, who was nicknamed "the Red Devil," it was outfitted with two 68-horsepower electric motors. It won its race and shattered the previous land-speed record, hitting 105.88 km/h (65.79 mph).

DAUPHINE CAR

The Dauphine was a car built by the Renault company between 1956 and 1967. It was an immediate and immense success with the middle class and contributed greatly to the automobile boom in France. A comfortable family car, it could reach 71 mph (115 km/h).

FARMAN MF 11BIS BIPLANE

The first motorized flight dates from the beginning of the twentieth century. Numerous prototypes—from the simple glider to the monoplane, with the biplane in between—went through testing in Europe and the United States. In France, the army quickly saw the military potential of the biplane. The MF11, built by the Farman brothers, was one of the first combat aircraft used by the French army in World War I. Outfitted with a propeller and a light steel frame, it could hold a pilot and a passenger and fly faster than 68 mph (110 km/h).

INDO-PACIFIC SAILFISH

As you might guess, the Indo-Pacific sailfish is found in the Indian and Pacific Oceans and gets its name from the shape of its characteristic dorsal fin. Capable of reaching a speed of 68 mph (110 km/h), it is the world's fastest fish and is much quicker than the dolphin (25 mph [40 km/h]) and the orca (34 mph [55 km/h]).

130 KM/H
80 MPH

THE ZEPPELIN *HINDENBURG*

Built in 1936 to fly a route between Europe and the United States, the *Hindenburg* was the largest of all zeppelins, at 804 feet (245 m) long. It was capable of reaching an altitude of 820 feet (250 m) and had a cruising speed of 79 mph (127 km/h)—and could reach 84 mph (135 km/h) with favorable winds. In 1937 it was destroyed by a fire that took only thirty-four seconds to engulf the entire balloon.

MOTORCYCLE

The motorcycle was introduced in the late nineteenth century and became more widely available during World War I. In the 1960s, different kinds of motorcycles were developed: powerful sport bikes, more comfortable touring bikes, and rugged off-road bikes. While some bikes are equipped with a motor as powerful as the one found in a Formula 1 racecar (which can go 230 mph [370 km/h]), speed limits prevent motorcycles from going anywhere near that fast.

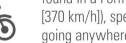

SWIFT

The swift is a small migratory bird often mistaken for a swallow. It is found throughout the world, except in the polar regions. Thanks to the pointed shape of its wings, the swift is . . . well, quite swift. It can fly at 93 mph (150 km/h) in pursuit, and at up to 125 mph (200 km/h) when diving at prey. It has few winged predators other than the peregrine falcon.

HUGHES MD 500 HELICOPTER

First thought up in the fifteenth century by Leonardo da Vinci, the helicopter didn't become a reality until the twentieth century. Propelled by rotors and various motors, the helicopter can take off and land vertically and can hover. Speed varies greatly, depending on the model of helicopter. The Hughes MD 500 can race through the sky at 125 mph (200 km/h).

CAUDRON SIMOUN TOURING PLANE

The Caudron Simoun was a French touring plane. In the 1930s it was used as a transport and training plane by the French air force, and also as a mail plane. Equipped with a six-cylinder engine, it was capable of an average speed of 168 mph (270 km/h). The Caudron Simoun was made famous by the French writer Antoine de Saint-Exupéry (the author of *The Little Prince*) in his novels *Night Flight* and *Wind, Sand and Stars*.

DOWNHILL SKIER

For a long time considered simply a mode of transportation, skiing became a winter sport at the end of the nineteenth century. Introduced in the Alps and other European mountain ranges, it became wildly popular in 1924, with the inauguration of the first winter Olympic Games, which brought together various winter sports, including downhill skiing, one of the fastest non-motorized sports. In 2006, the world speed record for a downhill skier was set at 156 mph (251 km/h).

TENNIS BALL

With its introduction in the 1870s, modern tennis rapidly became popular. Numerous tournaments are held each year in the United States, Great Britain, France, and Australia. Originally tennis balls were made of hard leather, but they didn't bounce very well. The speed record for a tennis ball off a serve is around 155 mph (250 km/h).

HIGH-SPEED TRAIN

Well into the twentieth century, trains were pulled by steam locomotives. Gradually steam locomotives ceded their place to electric locomotives, and then to diesel ones, whose power and performance have continued to improve. In France—where high-speed rail is widespread—the first such trains entered service in 1981, traveling at a speed of 200 mph (320 km/h). Soon it will be possible to travel from Paris to Bordeaux in only two hours—rather than the sixty it used to take by stagecoach!

PEREGRINE FALCON

The peregrine falcon is a bird of prey famous for being the fastest bird in the world. Found throughout the world, it nests on the slopes of mountains. The gull, the raven, the owl, and also the swift—itself known for great speed—are the peregrine's favorite prey. While a pigeon will struggle to reach 56 mph (90 km/h), the peregrine falcon can hit speeds equal to those of a Formula 1 car—scientists have clocked peregrines diving at 242 mph (389 km/h)!

FRIGATE BIRD

The frigate is a marine bird found in the tropics. Thanks to its large wings, whose span can reach 7.5 feet (2.3 m), it can fly for long distances without landing or getting tired. This veritable virtuoso of the air feeds on fish that it catches in midflight on the surface of the water or that it steals from other marine birds it attacks. A powerful hunter, it can dive at a fish at nearly 205 mph (330 km/h) without going into the water.

FORMULA 1 RACECAR

Formula 1 is a category of professional racing for single-seat racecars. The cars, which are built exclusively for the competition, have come to be known by the name "Formula 1." The ever-increasing power of their motors has allowed the cars to reach record speeds of greater than 230 mph (370 km/h) on a track.

500 KM/H
310 MPH

TORNADO

A tornado is a very powerful whirlwind that originates at the base of a storm cloud. Destructive meteorological phenomena, tornadoes are commonly encountered on most continents, including North America and Australia, and can move at over 60 mph (100 km/h) over thousands of miles. A force 5 tornado—the strongest category—can generate winds inside its vortex at speeds of nearly 310 mph (500 km/h).

1,000 KM/H
620 MPH

THE BLUE FLAME ROCKET CAR

The Blue Flame was an experimental car equipped with a rocket engine fueled by a mixture of hydrogen peroxide and natural gas. In 1970, it set a land speed record of 1,014 km/h (630 mph), becoming the first land vehicle to exceed 1,000 km/h (620 mph)!

PASSENGER JET

A passenger jet carries people—generally between 200 and 450—over long distances and across continents and oceans, at an altitude of more than 32,800 feet (10,000 m) and a cruising speed around 590 mph (945 km/h). They make it possible to go from New York to Paris in only six hours, rather than the six days needed for an ocean liner.

THRUST SSC TURBOJET CAR

The Thrust SSC is a supersonic car that set the current land speed record of 763.035 mph (1,227.985 km/h). Equipped with two afterburning turbojet engines, the Thrust is capable of going from 0 to 60 mph (100 km/h) in 1.6 seconds. It was the first wheeled vehicle to break the sound barrier.

1,700 KM/H
1,056 MPH

BULLET

The speed of a bullet shot from a pistol varies based on the bullet's composition, the weapon that fired it, and the air and environment. A bullet from a Magnum 9mm can reach a speed of 1,473 feet per second (449 meters per second), or more than 994 mph (1,600 km/h), breaking the sound barrier, which accounts for the big boom when the trigger is pulled.

THE EARTH'S ROTATION

The Earth was formed 4.6 billion years ago. The ancient Greeks were the first people to assert that the Earth is round, a fact that was confirmed in the 1520s by the great voyage of the Portuguese navigator Ferdinand Magellan, who circumnavigated the globe. The Earth, in rotation around its axis, spins at an average speed of 1,038 mph (1,670 km/h).

3,500 KM/H
2,175 MPH

BLACKBIRD SPY PLANE

The Blackbird (sometimes called the Habu, after a poisonous black snake) is a superfast airplane. Used by the U.S. military for photographic espionage and surveillance during the Cold War, it can exceed 2,190 mph (3,530 km/h)—or more than three times the speed of a passenger jet and nearly ten times that of a Formula 1 racer.

40,000 KM/H
25,000 MPH

APOLLO 11 SPACECRAFT

In 1969, *Apollo 11* was the first manned spacecraft to land on the Moon. It was propelled into space by the rocket *Saturn V*, which reached the speed of sound in one minute. Once the rocket was in orbit around the Earth, the *Apollo 11* spacecraft separated and broke free of the Earth's gravity, moving at a speed of 24,606 mph (39,600 km/h). Free of the Earth's pull, the craft cruised to the Moon at a leisurely pace of 3,418 mph (5,500 km/h)!

100,000 KM/H
60,000 MPH

SHOOTING STAR

In its voyage around the Sun, the Earth moves through regions swarming with meteors. More commonly called shooting stars, meteors enter the Earth's atmosphere at a speed of 63,000 to 160,000 mph (102,000 to 258,000 km/h). As a result, they reach a temperature of more than 3,630°F (2,000°C), and start to shine brightly at an altitude of 70 miles (115 km) before burning up completely.

Cataloging-in-Publication Data has been applied for and may be obtained from the Library of Congress.

ISBN: 978-1-4197-1338-5

Copyright © 2013 Gallimard Jeunesse

Originally published in French in 2013 under the title À Toute Vitesse! by Gallimard Jeunesse / Giboulées.

Printed and bound in China
10 9 8 7 6 5 4 3 2 1

Abrams Books for Young Readers are available at special discounts when purchased in quantity for premiums and promotions as well as fundraising or educational use. Special editions can also be created to specification. For details, contact specialsales@abramsbooks.com or the address below.

ABRAMS
THE ART OF BOOKS SINCE 1949
115 West 18th Street
New York, NY 10011
www.abramsbooks.com